Human's Cries

Neethu Susan Koshy

In loving memory of Dad,

trust me, this is just the beginning.

notionpress.com

INDIA • SINGAPORE • MALAYSIA

ISBN
Paperback 979-8-89475-965-4
Hardcase 979-8-89556-812-5

Acknowledgments

To my family:

Thank you to my parents for taking care of me throughout these 15 years. I would like to extend my gratitude to them as they have had to endure me and all my little stupid shenanigans. From taking me to many classes and meeting all my demands to listening to all the drama in my life about boys, friendships and more; they have suffered more than any other parents I believe.

To my cousins:

Thank you for picking up the call no matter how busy you are with studies and other extracurriculars. Mostly, I'm truly grateful about the fact that you both helped me get back to reality whenever I was going astray. I would request both of you to stay strong just like you told me. Lastly, thank you for being a brother figure for me.

To my grandparents:

Thank you for always being there for me and also thank you for saving me from getting any scoldings by my parents due to my little pranks. Also thank you for helping me in my weak subjects and celebrating every small win of mine.

To my relatives:

Thank you for always believing in me and helping me throughout these wonderful and extraordinary fifteen years.

To my friends:

How can I forget all of you! You all have been there to tease me and make sure I'm thoroughly embarrassed every single day. Most of all I really thank you for reading my poems and being the inspiration for a few of the poems in the book. I wish you the best for all your future endeavors.

To my best friend:

Thank you for being with me since we were 5. I don't even want to think how my life would have been if you never came into it. You always know how to cheer me up and I love the fact that I can just talk to you and tell you everything as if you are my personal diary. Now, since you have shifted to Mumbai, I don't think I will get to see you for a long time but that is ok cause one phone call a week is enough....

To myself:

Thank you Neethu for not giving up on your dream. I know writing this book and the poems took more than a year but I'm so grateful that you continued with your passion. I hope everything you manifested for this year and all your dreams come true. Most of all I hope you make it great in your life.

Contents

POEMS

LOVE

POEMS

LOVE

LOVE

- Ep 1: Loved Too Much
- Ep 2: Non Existent
- Ep 3: Flew away
- Ep 4 : Smile
- Ep 5: Hate
- Ep 6: Nameless
- Ep 7: Who's First
- Ep 8: De – Everything
- Ep 9: BFFs of GFs
- Ep 10: Signals
- Ep 11: Never
- Ep 12: Kneel
- Ep 13: Lover
- Ep 14 : Almost
- Ep 15: The screen
- Ep 16: Destination
- Ep 17: Vie
- Ep 18: Romance is dead
- Ep 19: Attracted
- Ep 20: Coffee stained letters

Ep 1: Loved Too Much

What wrong have I done,

Loving you with all my heart.

For now I love none...

For you played my Heart with darts.

Started being friends,

To having feelings,

Now our line has come to an end;

For cause of you my heart is peeling

AWAY.

Done and Dusted with you,

Yet some tiny sparks.

Every time I see you,

Poisonous, deadly marks....

CARVED IN MY HEART.

Your charming smile,
Turned into the deadly Nile.
Your crystal eyes,
Now is questioning me.
Why?

You treated me like dirt,
Expecting me to be okay with it.
I'll now be curt,
Your words.....it hurt me.

I loved you too much.
I hate myself for doing so....

Now I'm a duchess
Need no help and pity.
Nothing.
No.

For now I found the pieces of my heart
With which I loved too much.

Ep 2: Non Existent

I guess you don't know me,
I guess it's fine,
I guess I'll let you be,
Even if you exploit my soul like a gold mine.

Without even knowing, you cast a spell on me,
I fell into a trance,
Every morning, night and soiree,
Thinking with you, I have a chance.

I see you with her,
I feel so sad,
I feel like murdering her,
I know, I'm......bad.

Your glasses,
Your serious face,
Your quiet self and
Your funny self.

What wrong have I done,

Loving you so much.

My heart beats like a gong,

Now I can't escape your clutch.

You barely even know me.

You would probably even think
of me as a random junior.

You probably hate me.

You would probably never even talk.

You may not know me,

But I still like you,

But I'll let you be,

As..........

You may not know me,

I must part ways.

Ep 3: Flew away

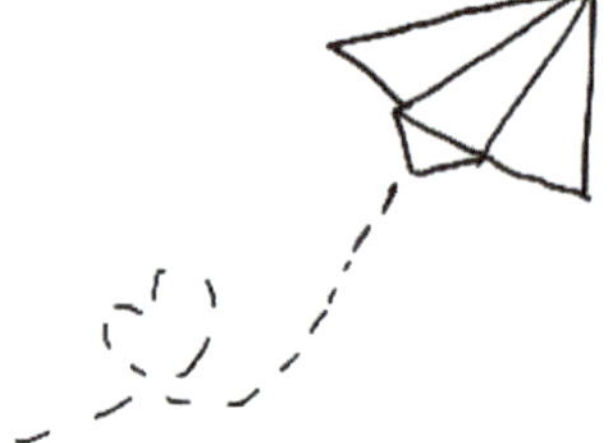

5 years ago,

Wow, half a decade.

There you were, next to me.

Must be destiny.

A Bond for 2 years,

Set my heart on fire.

Then, you were right here,

But, Now, No more.

Things I did for you,

Uncountable,

I got myself to read mythological books.

Something my mind would not have been available for.

I spent minutes and hours,

Listening to your woes.

Now, I am done.

My hopes flew away like Noah's dove.

Now you're long gone,

Living your life in another country.

Probably with no clue about me,

But my heart still is lingering for you.

I guess I can say that My heart flew away with you.

Ep 4: Smile

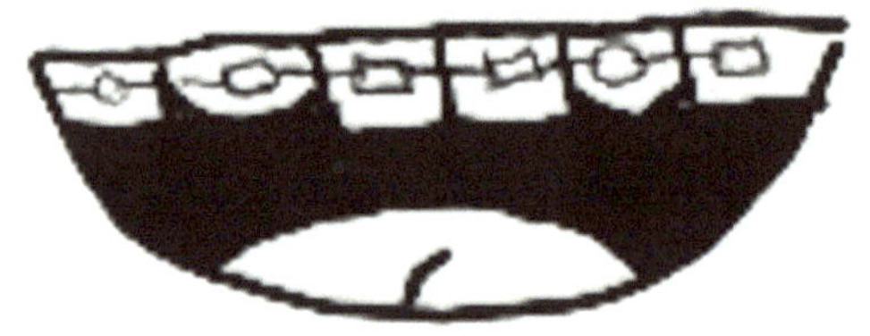

You are taken (I guess),
I am absolutely broken.
Now my heart is shattered,
Into pieces,
The pieces are scattered.

Never mind.

I see you with your 'Homies',
And then I see your smile,
....Your faint smile.

But I see you with her,
The love of your life (I guess),
And only then do I see your smile,
.....Your wide smile.

That very Smile,
That Happy smile,
That genuine and sincere smile,
That 'Lovely smile which shows your braces' smile.

When will that
Ever be shown to me.

Well you don't know me (I guess),
I'll let you and your charming smile be.
Hoping it will be shown to me,
At Least once in this lifetime.

I bid Adieu,
to you and her, especially your smile.

Ep 5: Hate

I hate you,

I really do.

I really hate you.

I hate her too, your girlfriend.

I hate that you are still together.

I hate that I have to see you both
talking and holding hands,

EVERY DAY.

I hate your charming smile,

I hate your thick rimmed glasses,

I hate your dark and creepy music,

I hate your friends,

I hate how they don't know that,

I LIKE YOU.

I Hate how I see you every other day,

I hate seeing you in competitions,

I hate see you laugh,

I hate your personality,

I hate that I want to hate everything about you.

But,

I hate that you give me butterflies
without even knowing,

I hate that day when I talked to you,

I hate that I liked you.

But Mainly,

I hate that I still like you, even if

I tell myself not to.

Ep 6: Nameless

Saw you twice,
I guess it was a game of dice.
A chance.
I don't know your name,
Neither the name of your lovely dame,
If any.

Let's be honest,
You were the sweetest,
You gave me hope in love again,
Now with the devil I must bargain.

We first met under the holy cross,
I couldn't resist my temptation and I know,
with me the Lord is cross.

Next, I see you with your friends.
Don't know their names either.

You saw me there.
You saw my messages.
You saw how I was talking to my friends about you.
You saw those tomato cheeks of mine.

WHEN TALKING ABOUT YOU.

You too don't know me,
It's fine, I'm used to it.
Nameless you are and
Clueless I am.

I SHALL NAME YOU 'R

Ep 7: Who's First

I wanted the crown,

But you wanted to see me in a wedding gown.

Ep 8: De – Everything

For you the badge I risked,

But for me nothing was risked....

Ep 9: BFFs of GFs

You were freely drawing,

And I was drying..

My wet, soaked heart

Which absorbed all my tears

From knowing you love me not.

Ep 10: Signals

Yes or a No,

Or probably a, Go

AWAY.

It's always,

"Your annoying",

"What are you shouting for",

"Blah blah blah".

A gesture.

A clue.

A signal.

Nothing No.

Do you like me or,

Am I fantasizing about it?

You neither hint to me,

Nor wink at me.

I guess I'm fantasizing,

Hallucinating.

A dream from which

I'll soon wake up.

Ep 11: Never

I was the stalker,

and

You were my lover.

You were the thief,

and

I was the sheriff,

Running after you in circles.

I was the soil,

and

You were the rain,

Making me feel alive and fresh.

I was the forest,

and

You were the fire,

Burning my heart alive.

I was the painter,

and

You were my muse,

And boy, what a masterpiece I drew!

But this was what I thought,
It was what I sought,
FOR.

You were really handsome,
But only for some.
I only watched you from afar,
And I must say, you are by far,
THE BEST.

Well I can't keep running after you,
And I must let that tide in my heart subdue.

As you were NEVER mine and NEVER will be.

Ep 12: Kneel

Just like you kneeled down for the flag,
Would you kneel down for me too?

Ep 13: Lover

I may have the product,

But she has the mark.

And, I will forever be jealous of that...

Ep 14: Almost

If there is one word
from the dictionary
I must choose
I would choose **almost**

Almost.
The most excruciating, hurtful and deadly word.
That word which is even heard by the dead soul.
It is that one word which will never be unheard,
And will bring your life into the black hole.

For,
He **almost** lived.
She **almost** won.
I **almost** passed.
They **almost** had a child.
She **almost** converted into a nun.
He was **almost** harassed...

But, for me,
I almost had him.
He almost tried to love me.
We were almost about to date,
Until SHE came.

And this time, there was no 'almost'.
For,
She loved him.
And he loved her back.
They dated.
They got married.

And there I was.
Standing next to that oak tree,
Near my house,
On which we once carved our initials.

It's still there,
What a miracle.

Ep 15: The screen

You don't know me,
I don't know you,
But we talk through,
The screen.

I have studied your facial features,
Memorized your laugh,
Listened to your soothing voice,
Uncountable times,
Through,
The screen.

I know I'll never see you,
I know you'll never know me,
I know you'll never memorize me,
Like I did.

But,
I know you'll hopefully see me through,
The screen.

Ep 16: Destination

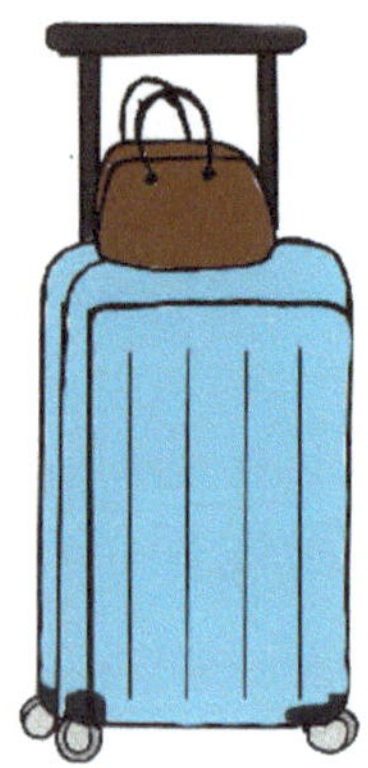

A million humans with luggages,
With different destinations.

Will I ever find my one true man,
Well, my one true boy,
With the same destination as me?

Ep 17: Vie

C'est la vie!
Yes this is truly life!
Loving you,
Admiring you from afar.
Watching you pursue,
YOUR dreams,
And celebrating your first paycheck at a bar.

C'est la vie!
Truly you are the epitome of my life.
You are the reason I'm living.
And I hope to be your wife,
For the rest of my life.

C'est la vie.

Finding out you never loved me.

Finding out we will just be friends.

Finding out that there will never be an 'us'.

Finding out that this is where
our friendship may descend.

C'est la vie!

Yes, this is truly life!

Knowing that I never needed you in the first place.

And that I can do quite well on my own.

Knowing that you will be replaced in my life,

By someone unknown.

C'est la vie!

Ep 18: Romance is dead

You were the definition,

Meaning,

Epitome,

And a lovely example of love.

But now romance is dead.

And so are you.

Ep 19: Attracted

Let's make something clear.
I'm attracted to you,
But only when you suddenly appear.
Cause you are truly quite a view!

I never want to experience 'love' with you,
Cause I really don't like you,
I am just attracted to you.

I never want to shower you with compliments,
Cause I really don't like you,
I am just attracted to you.

I never want to go on dates with you,
I never want to hug you at the end of the day,
Nor behind the bus bay,
Cause,
I am just attracted to you.

I'll be curt and honest,
I don't like nor love you,
I am just attracted to you.
I just admire your chiseled face.
Your chocolate brown orbs and
Your messy bed hair.

I AM JUST ATTRACTED TO YOU
AND
THIS WILL NEVER BE LOVE!
(but why?....)

Ep 20: Coffee stained letters

Words are like flowers.

Sweet,

Precious,

And unique, made out of a few letters from the set.

But words are also like dumbbells.

Heavy,

Painful,

And tear jerking causing waterfalls to spurt out
of my dark licorice black orbs.

Nevertheless, words are like clowns.

Funny,

Quirky,

And amusing, never failing to bring out my best smile.

I want all of these words,

all jumbled up in a letter.

Not just any letter.

...

I want a coffee stained letter,

Letter which looks burned at the edges,

The letter with scribbles and tears stains.

The letter which is written by my lover……………

But, I don't have one,

Guess I have to write one for myself,

But that is no fun.

For

I would refuse to believe a word written there,

I would scoff at my compliments,

And no words could bring a smile to my face.

CAUSE…

I loathe myself.

And I believe I will only be loved by someone else.

SOMEONE I WILL NEVER FIND.

Friends

Friends

- Ep 1: Expired
- Ep 2: See you
- Ep 3: Competition
- Ep 4 : Toxic
- Ep 5: I Love you....OOPS

Ep 1: Expired

Why?

Just why!

Do you really like ignoring us that much,

Or do you just wanna be out of touch?

Truly and really just tell us.

Are you addicted to breaking hearts like its drugs,

Do you like shattering a soul,

Like it's a mine of gold.

"Oh, finally you wore something decent !"

"You look worse than me even with makeup !"

"That guy doesn't even know you, why bother?"

"You will ruin the photo because

you are the only one wearing pants."

Was that first handshake of ours fake?

Are you now purposely putting our friendship at stake?

Do you adore hurting people and their feelings?

Does our friendship even have a meaning?

Do you want to end the line in six months?

Can you please try to be courteous once..

Can you try at least,

Or has that chain been released.

Those lovely memories we made,

Have they faded?

I guess they have,

For everything I gave.

HAS NOW EXPIRED.

Ep 2: See you

6 A, B, C and

8 D, E.

Five seats.

Five people.

To a different state.

A decade,

120 months,

All spent together.

We watched each other grow up.

We watched each other lose our first tooth.

We went through different grades together.

We went through good and bad teachers together.

You've seen my delusional phases,

You've seen my lovesick phases,

You've seen me cry about my marks.

But mostly,

You've seen the wonderful memories
we made together.

I've seen your sports achievements,

I've seen you come late to class due to practice,

I've seen you being undermined
because of your siblings.

But mostly,

I've seen the wonderful memories we made together.

I truly and surely will miss you,

And I really don't want to let you go,

Mostly because of the memories we made.

But, its ok

For

It's always see you,

And never goodbye.

Ep 3: Competition

Life is to be enjoyed
And friends are to be cherished,
But NO.
Life is to be exploited and destroyed
And friendships are to be perished.

That's my life.
That's my warning.
That's my so-called 'toxic trait.'
But mainly,
That's my 'sole purpose' in life.

So beware,
You can't trust me,
You can love me.
For if you want to be free.
It's better not to be my friend, my dear.

I'll consider you as my competition,
In marks, looks and grades.
I'll take out my frustration out on you,
Just because of your marks.

Leaving now is the best idea,
Maybe never even meeting me,
Will be the best idea.
For
I don't have friends,
Only competitions.

Ep 4: Toxic

You're toxic.
And I hope you know that,
But of course.
I'll never leave you.
Cause I have no one else.

Ep 5: I Love you.... OOPS

Been caging these three words like a caged bird,
Yet the role of a true soulmate was what I served.
U didn't realize it,
U mistook it as friendship.

Made you your drip brewed coffee,
Made your day better with sunflower every day,
Wrote advices on your locker every day,
Wrote songs all about you and only you...

Many bloody acts of service!
Laced every word of mine with sugar and caramel.
Sweet enough to sugar coat you,
But again you mistook it as friendship.

I confessed and that's when I knew,
I messed up.

I confessed and that's when I knew,
Our line as friends ended.

I confessed and that's when I knew,
I'll never have you as a soul mate or even as a friend.

Remains of Someone

Remains of Someone

Ep 1: Earphones

My life.

My love.

My hope.

My escape route.

My earphones.

The doors help too,

Sometimes tho,

Cupping my ears with my hand,

It was that bad...

Shouting.

Yelling.

Screaming.

Crying.

It hurts my ears,

Every time, it hurts my dears too,

Earphone,

It tones down those bad omens,

Blast some music,

Probably some classic,

AND I'M SORTED FOR THE NIGHT.

Ep 2: Decisions

Please.

Please.

Please.

I'm not a prisoner,

Nor are you my visitor.

I can make my own decisions.

I have my own visions.

I can make it in this world.

I am not to be kept preserved.

I'm not your slave,
If so, please dig my grave.
RIGHT NOW!

I have my own opinions,
I am not one of your minions,
I can chase my own dreams,
I don't want to follow any of your schemes.

Please.
Please.
Please.

I'm a star,
And I am not to be enclosed in a jar.

I really can make my own decisions,
For I have my own unique visions...

Ep 3: The French flag

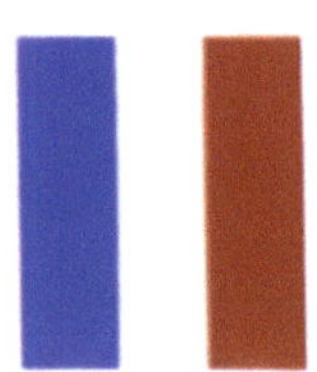

Two colors of the flag :

Red and blue.

Or as the french say :

Rouge et bleu.

These were the colors of my bruises,

My scars,

My blemishes,

Which soon took up the entire space in my face.

There were many causes to these marks:

Drunk nights,

Drugless nights,

Duty nights,

And also days.

People always ask why I own so much makeup,
People always call me a 'pick- me',
People always describe my makeup is 'cakey',
Ask me why and I say............

It's to cover up the french flag which has now left me unpatriotic to my own bloodline.

Ep 4: Mia's Mia

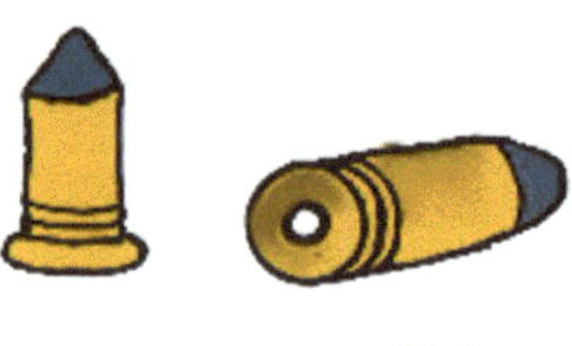

My name is Mia

And this is my parents' MIA story....

Cold nights,

When all the trees where leafless and lifeless,

I waited,

Just like I did every other fortnight.

This very eerie fortnight turned into the bright dawn,

Happiness and hopes turned into
despairs and cries for help.

This very fortnight turned into
the third hopeless night,

Joy and warmth turned into starvation and doom.

Fourth morning

The day the rays hit me,

The day it hit me,

The day I realized.

I had no pillars.

The two biggest boulders.

Who held me through every step,

With whom I survived till now,

Lay dead on the threshold.

With three bullets in the back,

One piercing their hearts....

Which undoubtedly broke and shattered
mine into shards and pieces.

Ep 5: What happened?

****

****

******

*****

You cursed me,

Day and night.

Why do you want to set these cruel words free?

Causing a huge fight,

Between us

Then you act as if nothing happened;

You ask "what happened"

....

WHAT HAPPENED

What happened is the fact that you cursed me,

Wished ME, YOUR OWN BLOODLINE well in hell

And you now pretend that you said
nothing abusive or hurtful.

While I hold back salty tears and prevent a
waterfall,

Cause we were in public

And I am no child to cry,

Or am I......

www.ingramcontent.com/pod-product-compliance
Lightning Source LLC
LaVergne TN
LVHW021331160826
845679LV00008B/1345
9798894759654